• CHARLOTTE'S FRECKLE

Author Mem Mills

Published 2014 through Createspace

ISBN: 13: 978-1502533326

Also as e-book with Kindle Books

- ***This author also writes as Mary Mills-Maclaren'***
- **The Four Elizabeths**
- **Elizabeth's NewLife**
- **Laura's Gold**
- **Short collections Flashes 1 + 2**

I was the biggest freckle on Charlotte's face.

And she hated me!

Even worse, it was the day before her birthday.

Her mother was in the kitchen icing the pink and white birthday cake, ready for the candles.

"You said this freckle would go away when I grew up, and I'm EIGHT tomorrow!" Charlotte complained.

"I can't always be right," said her mother. "And you can't always have everything your way."

"I know that," said Charlotte, giving a big sigh.

“I don’t want a party,” grumbled Charlotte.

“All your friends have been invited,” said Mother. “Even the new little girl who moved into the house across the road.”

“I don’t care,” said Charlotte.

“Stop being silly,” said Mother, who was very busy. “Now go and play while I finish your cake.”

Charlotte went to her room and gazed into the mirror.

I know I'm only a freckle, but I wished Charlotte wouldn't get so upset about me.

I think I'm rather cute.

Her next words made me shiver.

"I'm going to get a pair of scissors and cut it off!" she said

I was so happy when she changed her mind

Next morning, Mother and Dad woke Charlotte and called…

"Happy Birthday, Sweetheart!"

Then Mother gave her a lovely 'grown-up' doll

Dad said, "And here's a pair of trainer shoes for you, just like the ones your doll is wearing,"

When Charlotte came downstairs, there was her favourite breakfast

Scrambled eggs on brown bread toast

...and a bottle of tomato sauce.

Dad tried to draw a big **8** on her eggs.

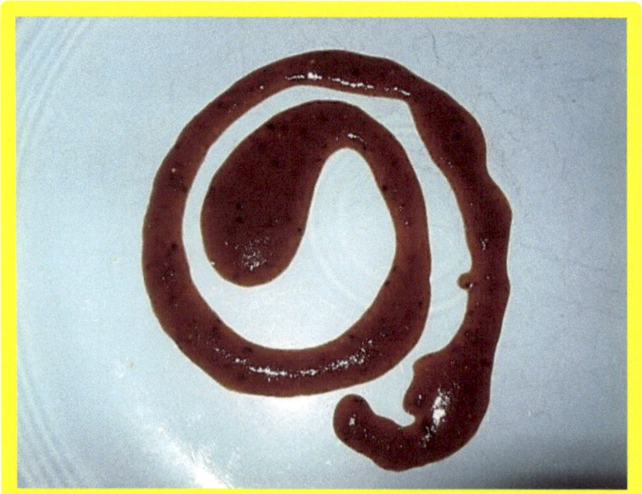

Well, I don't know. What do you think it looks like?

It sure doesn't look like a figure 8 to me!

But, I'm only Charlotte's Freckle, so I'm not supposed to know very much.

But, I will go on with my story… …

It was nearly time for the party guests to arrive.

Charlotte had a warm bath, which made her feel a lot better….

Then she went into her room to get dressed. At first, Charlotte couldn't decide what to wear. "It must be pink," she said, "to match Pixie!"

Charlotte had played Superwoman in school last year but she shook her head. Not quite right for a birthday party.

Then she dressed in pink, to match the new doll she'd named

PIXIE

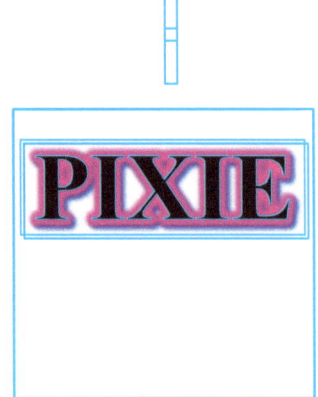

Charlotte felt very happy. She was eight years old today.
Then she looked closely in the mirror, and saw me, again.
Her face lit up, and I thought, 'Uh-oh!'

Charlotte began rummaging through her dressing table drawer.

She found lots of things she'd thought lost…

An old blue jumper…

...Bracelets

…Hair clips

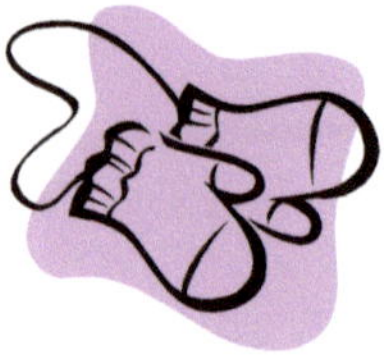

….Mittens

Finally, she said "Got one!"

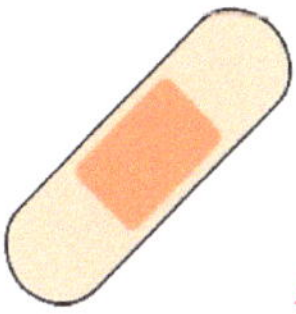

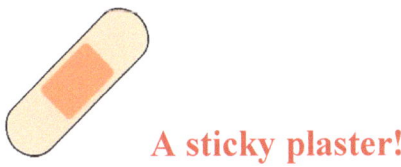

A sticky plaster!

…and when Charlotte stuck it over me, I couldn't see a thing.

Her friends,  nor her party……

or her birthday cake

"What have you done to your nose, Charlotte?" asked Mother.

"Oh, nothing," I heard Charlotte say, and I knew she was trying not to lie.

But she was saved when there was a knock on

the front door.

KNOCK! KNOCK!

As soon as mother opened the door, she said, "Well, hello", Melissa. Come in to the party room."

She called out as they walked in and said ,

"Everybody, this is our new neighbour, Mellissa!"

Charlotte smiled and said, welcome to my party,"

I COULD ONLY SEE HER LEGS, OF COURSE.

Then Charlotte surprised me and everyone, when she said, "Excuse me everyone, I'll be back soon,"

She went up to her room, and stripped the plaster off me

When Charlotte went back downstairs, all her guests began to sing…

Happy birthday to you…

Happy birthday to you…

Happy birthday dear Charlotte,

Happy birthday to you!

Charlotte said 'Thank You' politely, as you are supposed to, then blew out the candles and Mother took the cake into the kitchen to cut into pieces for them all.

Melissa sat oppositeo Charlotte, and said,

" I was eight the week before we moved here. "

"Ooh, good," said Charlotte. We'll be in the same class together and you can sit by me."

I wondered why Charlotte was being so friendly? Then I looked at Melissa closely, and there was a large brown freckle on her face, just like me!

Charlotte and Melissa have been the best of friends, ever since

www.ingramcontent.com/pod-product-compliance
Lightning Source LLC
Chambersburg PA
CBHW050927290526
45792CB00002B/915
9781502533326